That's Not Our Dog!

Story by Rose Inserra
Illustrations by Pat Reynolds

"Rex needs a bath," said Mom.
She looked at his long coat
and dirty paws.

"But he's too big for his bathtub,"
said Jacob.
"And he runs away
as soon as we get it out."

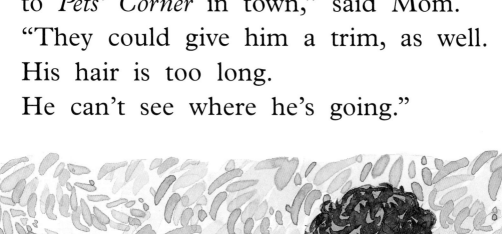

"We could take him
to *Pets' Corner* in town," said Mom.
"They could give him a trim, as well.
His hair is too long.
He can't see where he's going."

3

Mom and Jacob took Rex
to *Pets' Corner*.

"Come back for him this afternoon,"
said the man.

Jacob patted Rex.

The man took Rex away
and washed him.
Then he put him in a cage
that had a big blow-dryer.

5

When Rex was dry,
the man gave him a trim.

He cut off a lot of Rex's hair.

Then the man took Rex to another cage.
Rex was very tired,
and he went to sleep.

Mom and Jacob came back
in the afternoon.

"We have come to get our dog,"
said Jacob.

"What's his name?" asked the woman.

"He's called Rex," said Jacob.
"And he's a very **big** dog."

The woman walked over to the cages.
"Here's Rex," she said.
A big black dog stood up.

"But that's not our dog!" said Jacob.

"Isn't it?" said the woman.
"You had better come
and help me find him, then."

They walked along,
looking in all the cages.
There were big dogs and little dogs.
There were some sleepy dogs
that were too tired to move.

But they couldn't see Rex.

Inside the last cage
was a dog with spots.

"**That's** not our dog!" said Jacob.
"Rex hasn't got spots."

"He must be here somewhere,"
said the woman.
"We can't have lost him!"

"I know what we can do!" said Jacob.
"Rex loves going for walks.
Let's call out *Walk, Rex!*"

"Yes!" said Mom.
"He always runs to us and barks
when we say *Walk*."

Jacob ran along in front of the cages.
"Walk, Rex! Walk!" he called.

"Woof! Woof!" barked a dog.

"That sounds like Rex," cried Jacob.
"He must be over there.
But it doesn't look like him.
That dog's too thin."

Mom laughed.
"It **is** Rex," she said.
"Don't you remember?
We asked them to give him a trim!"

Jacob laughed, too.
"He doesn't look like Rex now.
That's why we didn't know him!"